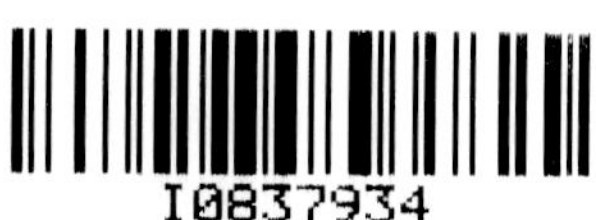

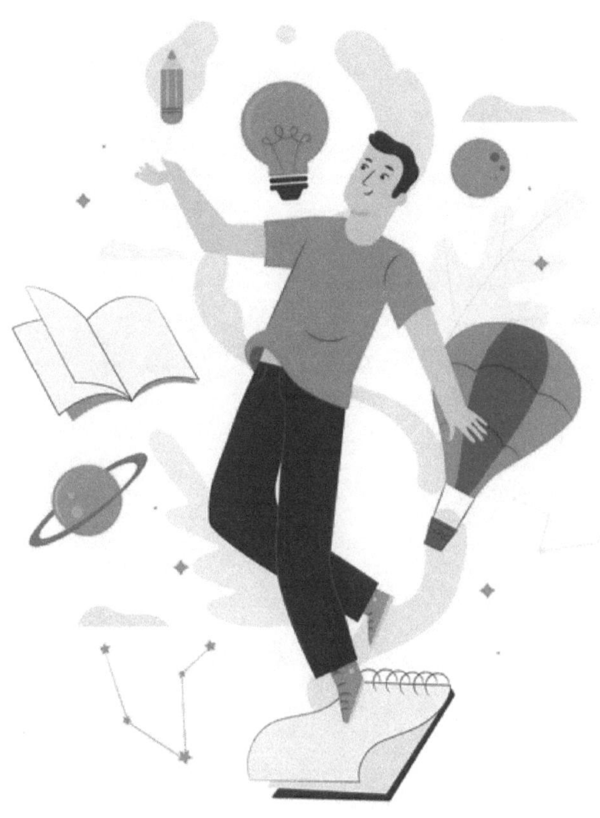

This coloring book belongs to:

____

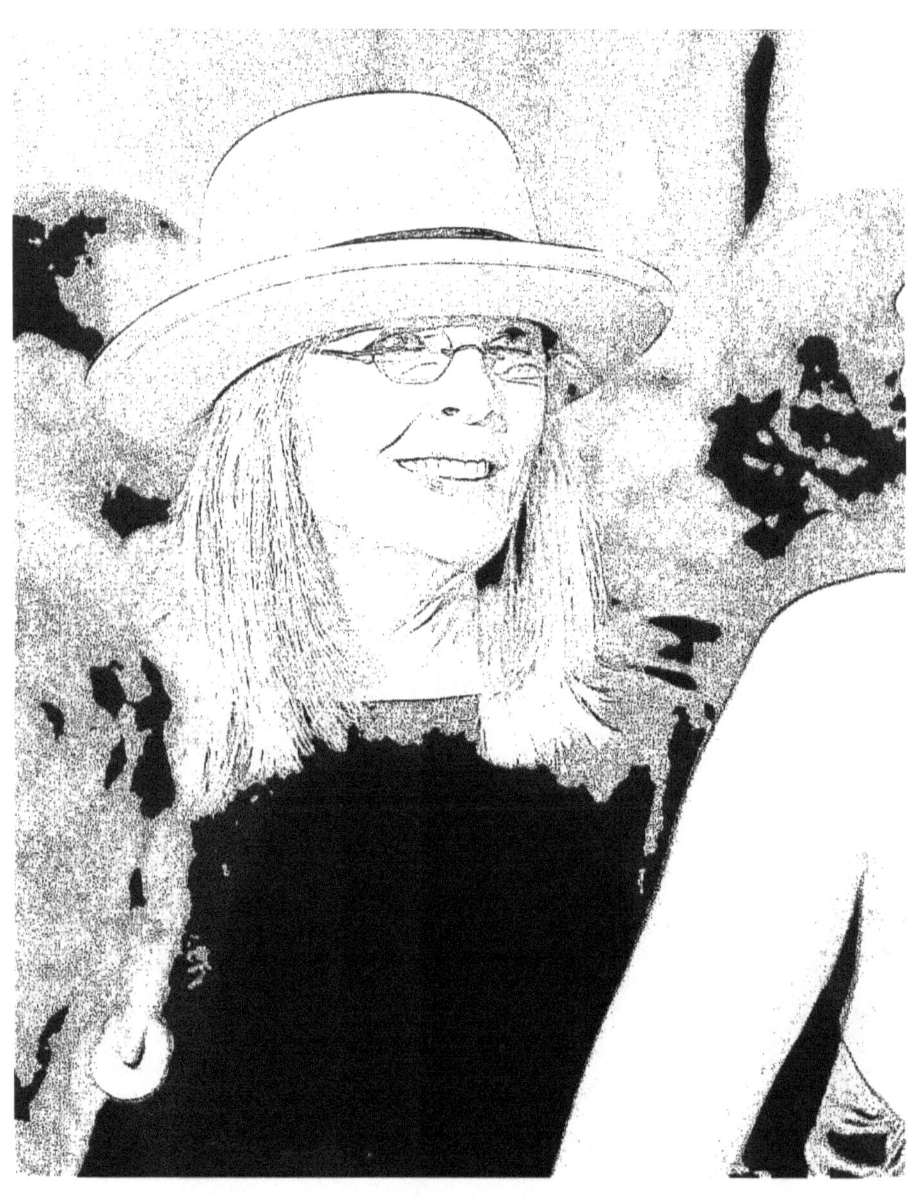

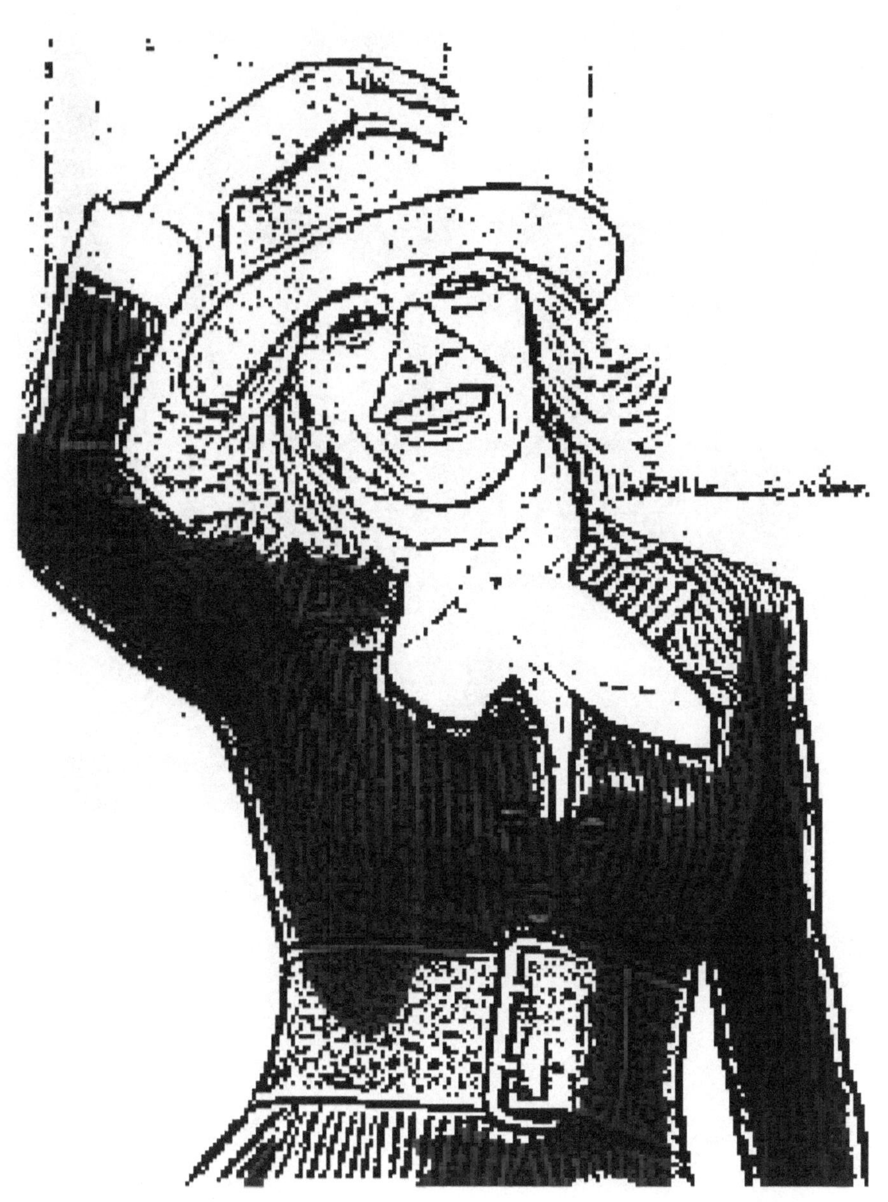

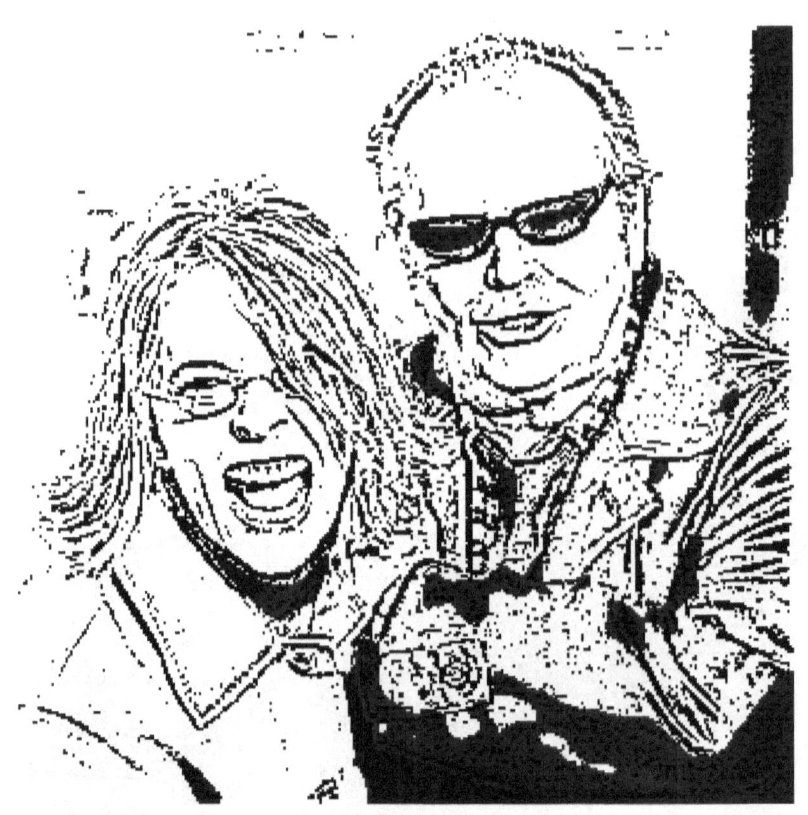

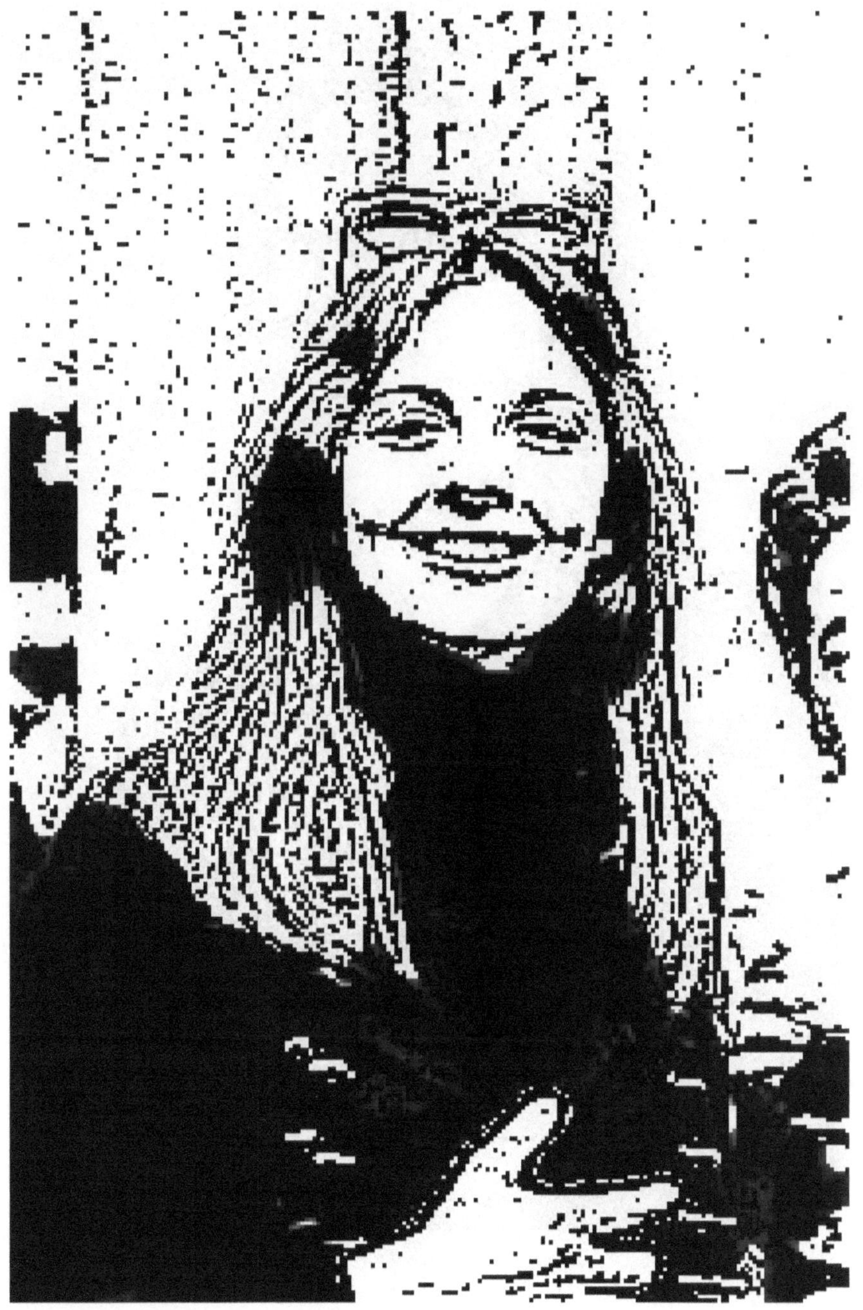

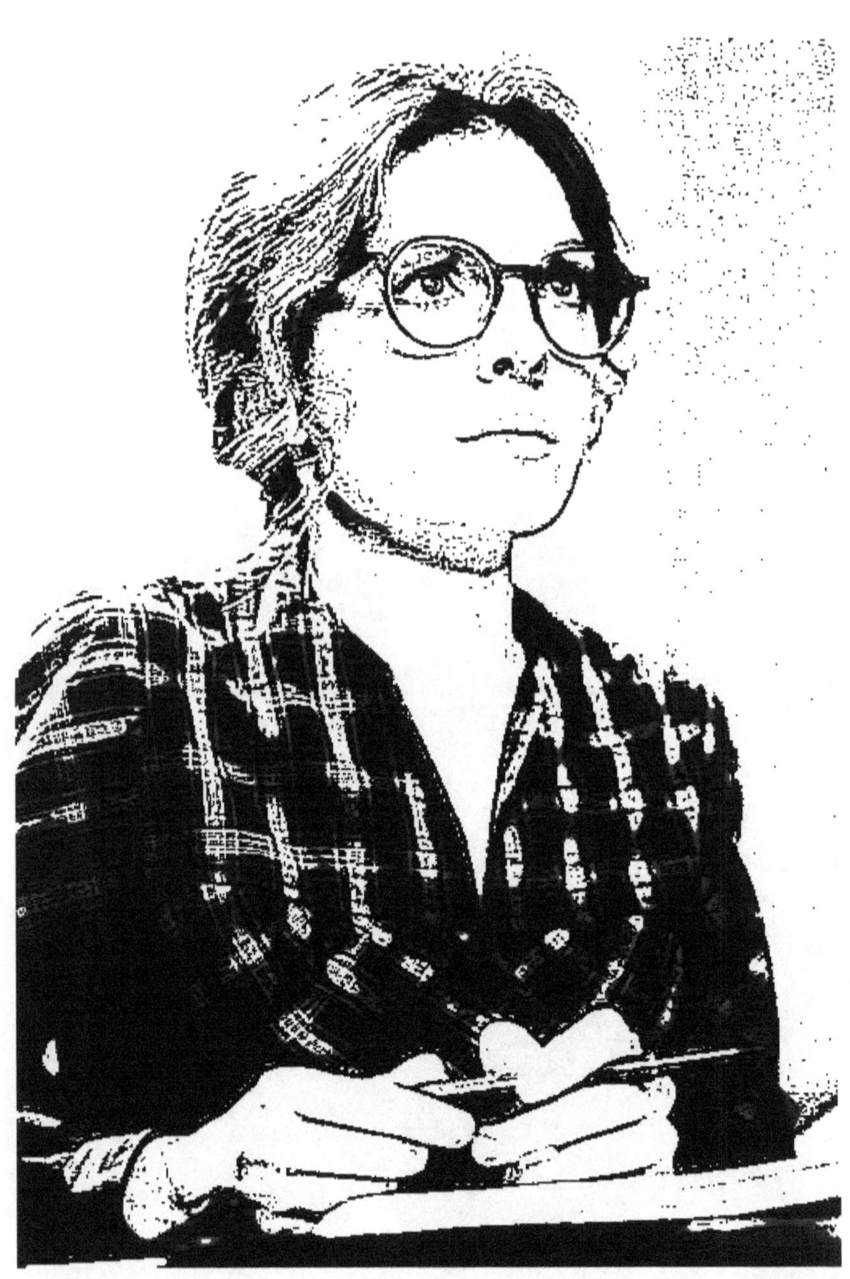

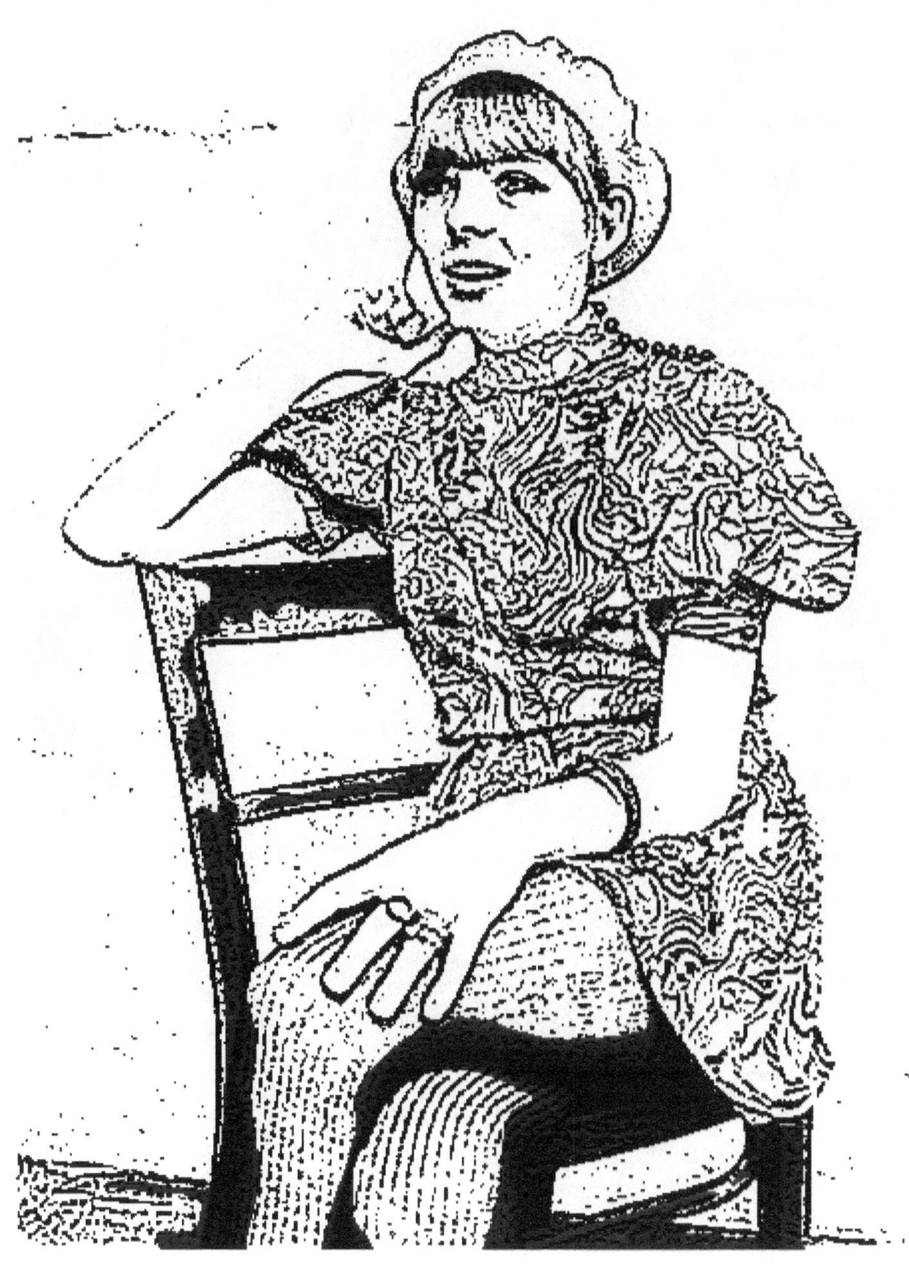

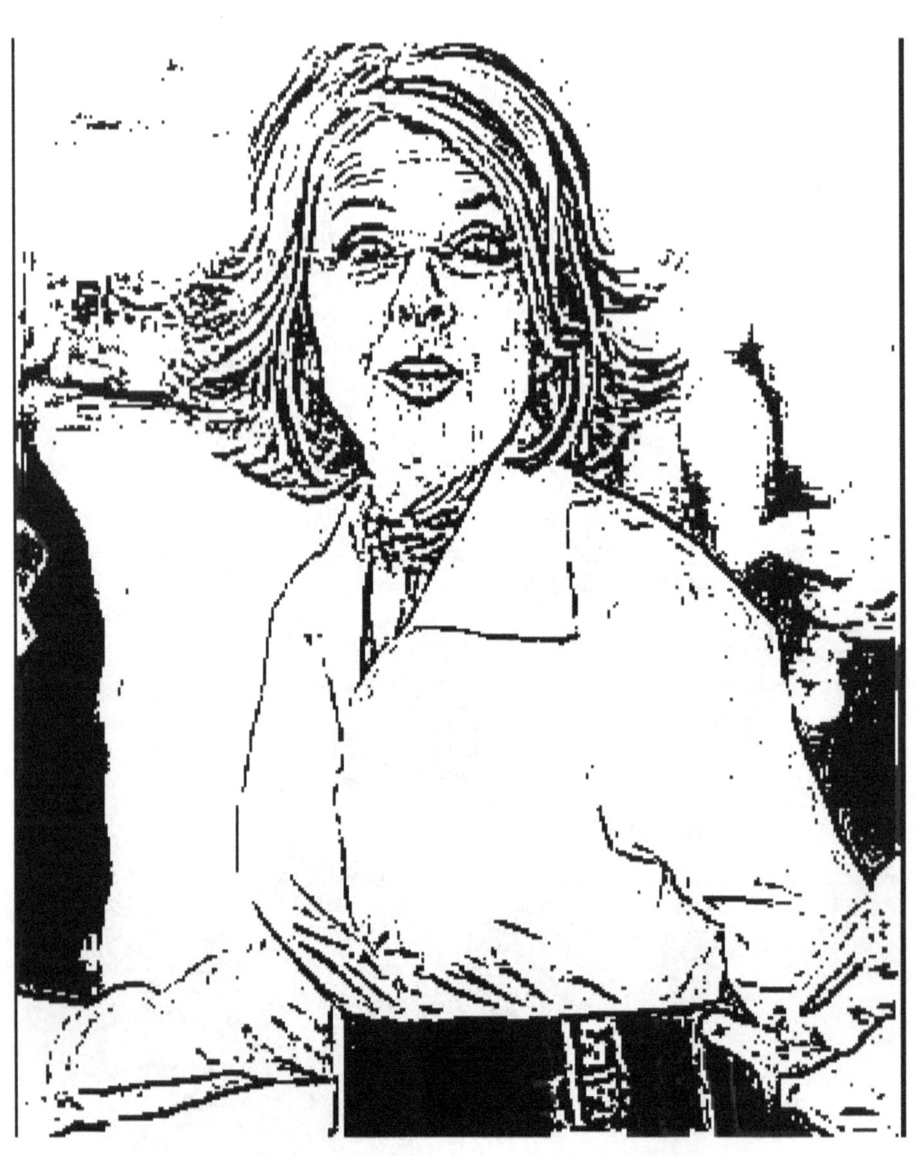

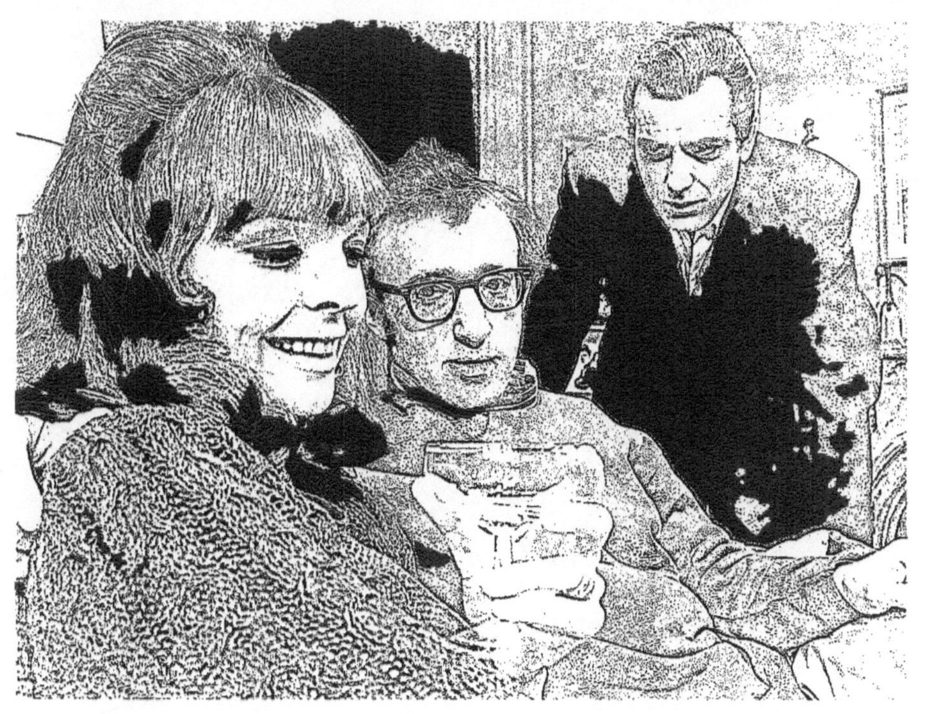

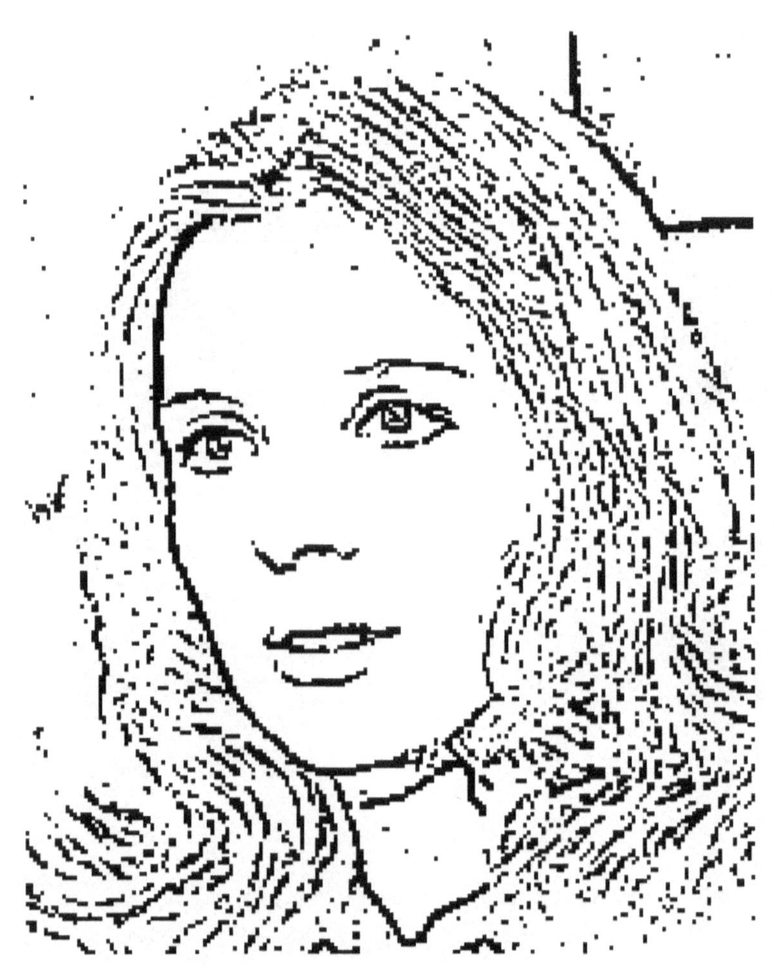

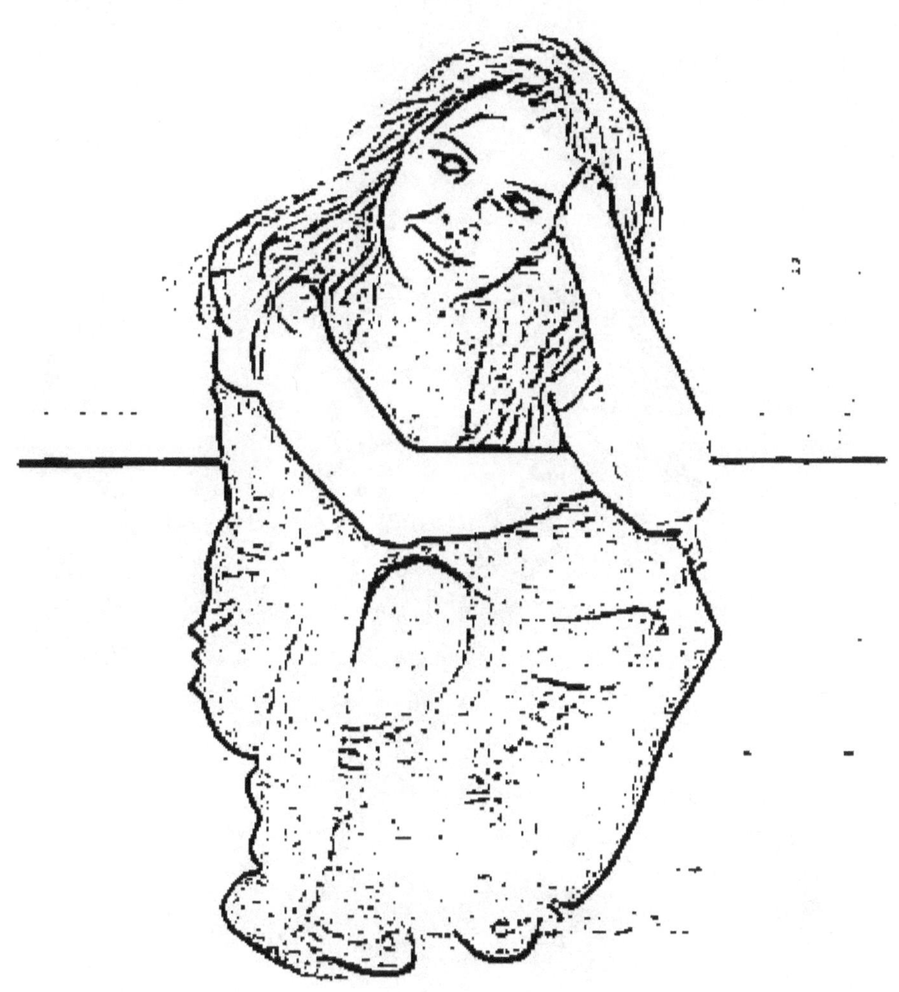

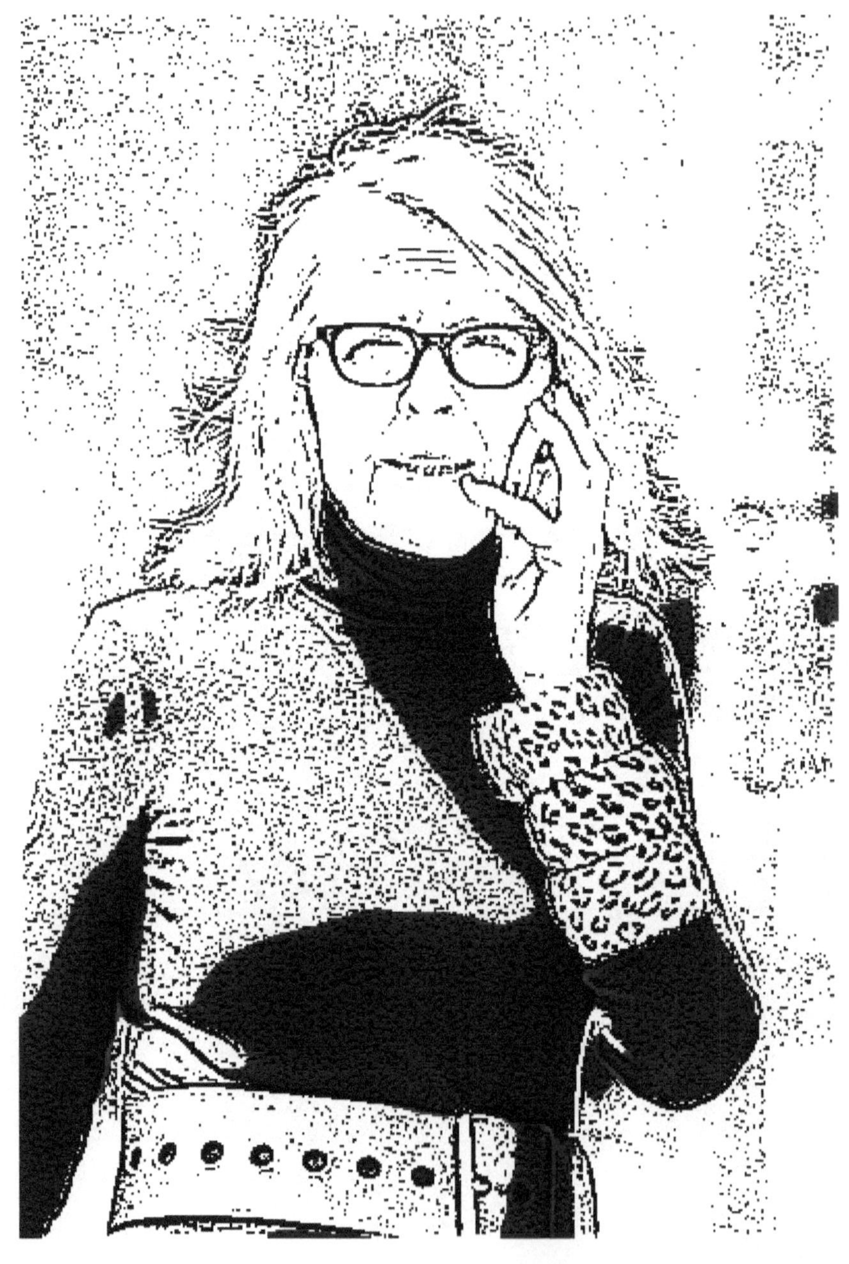

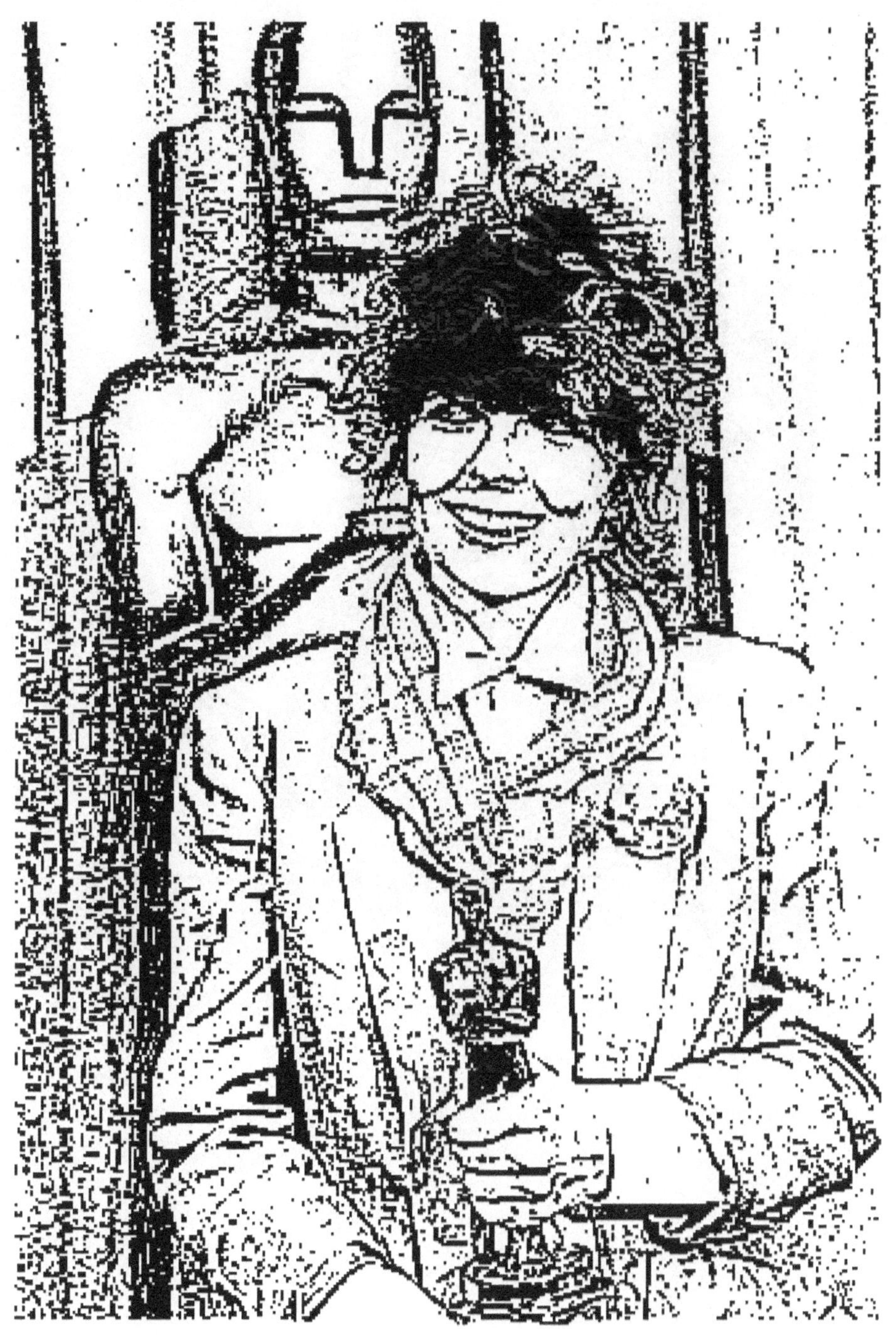

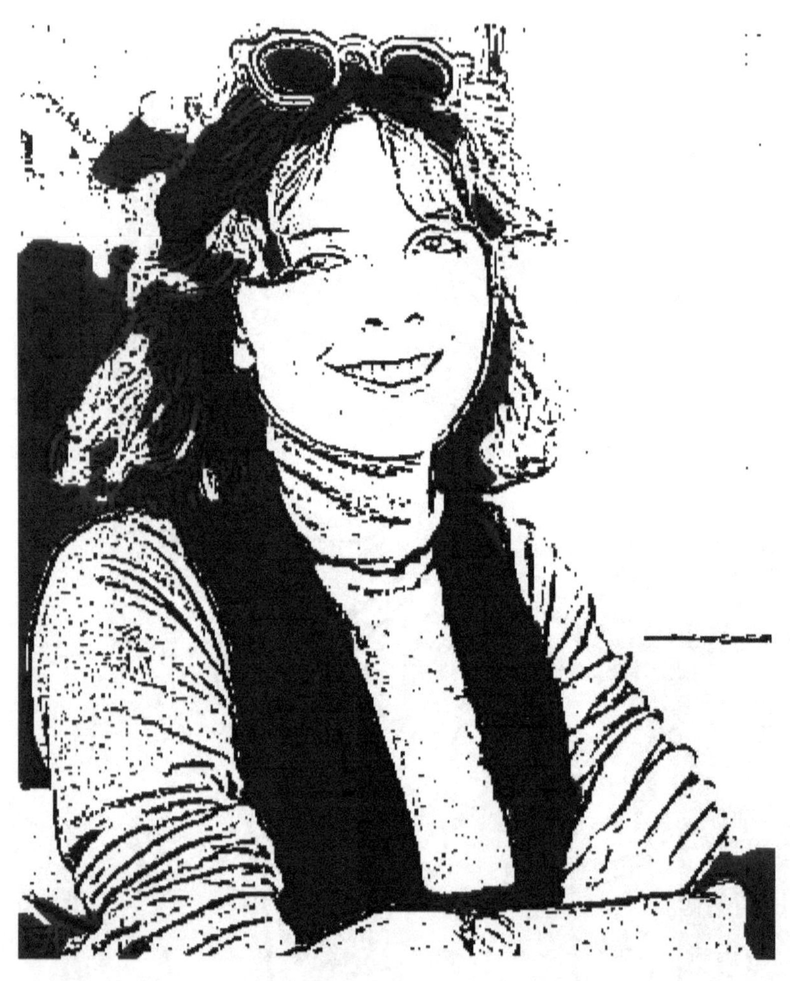

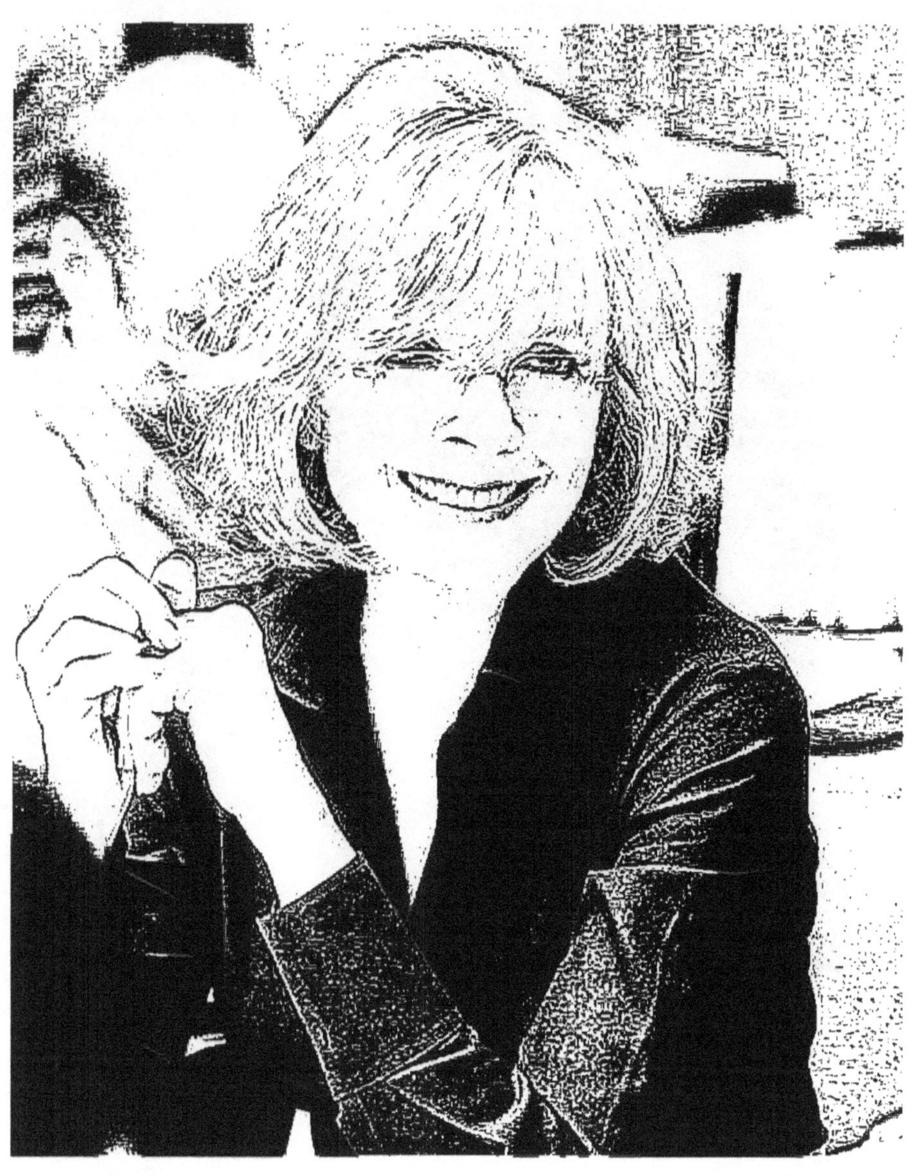

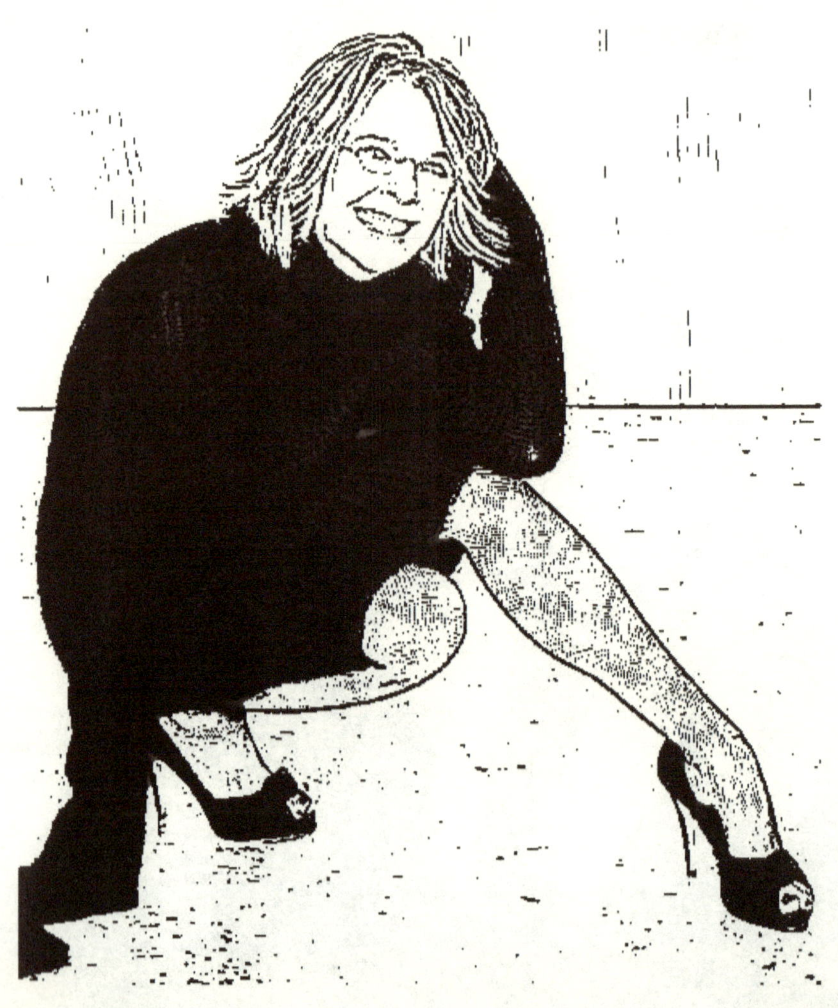

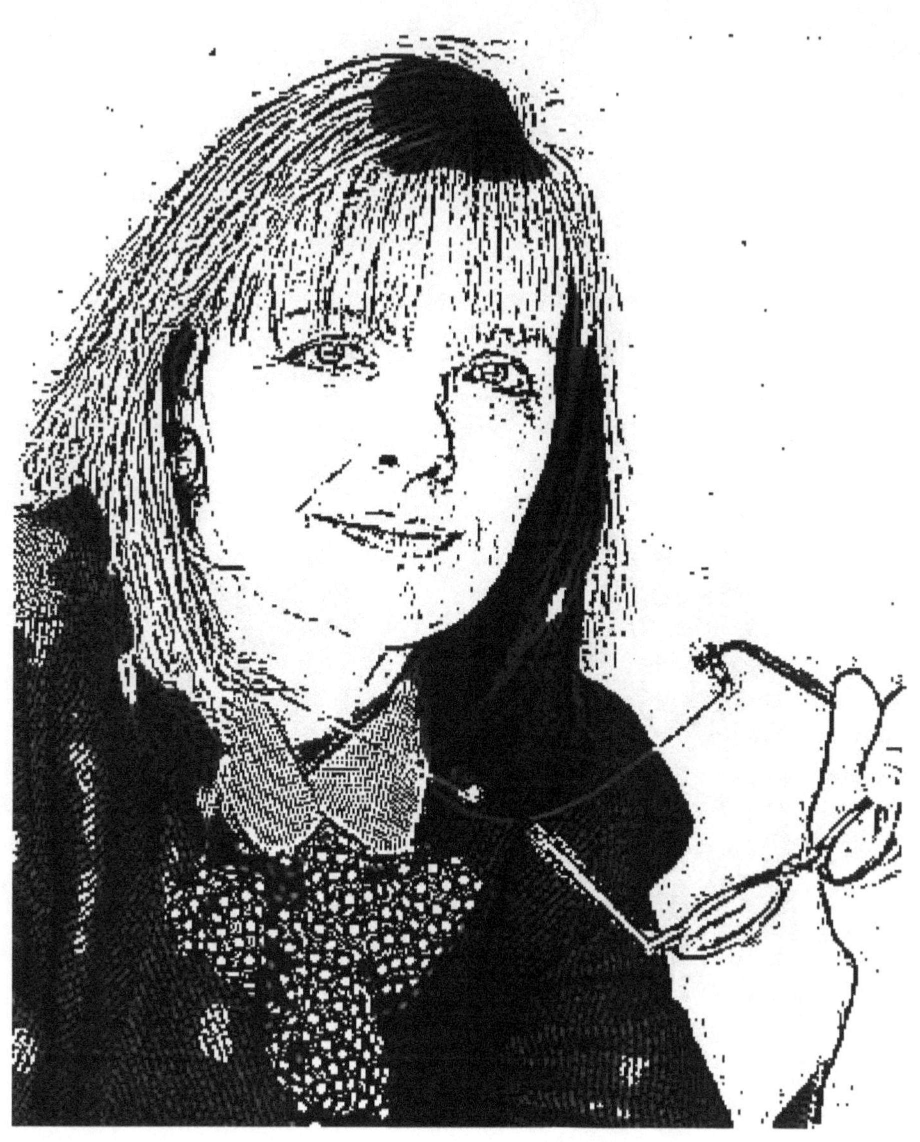

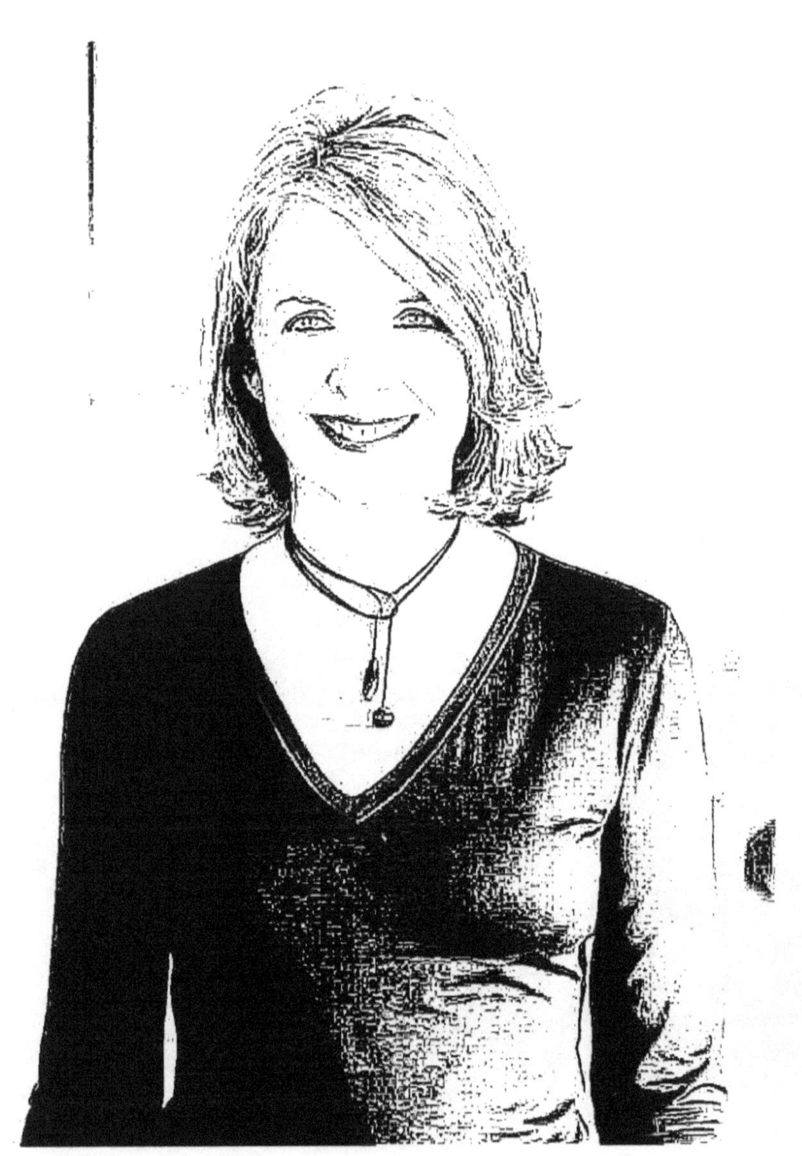

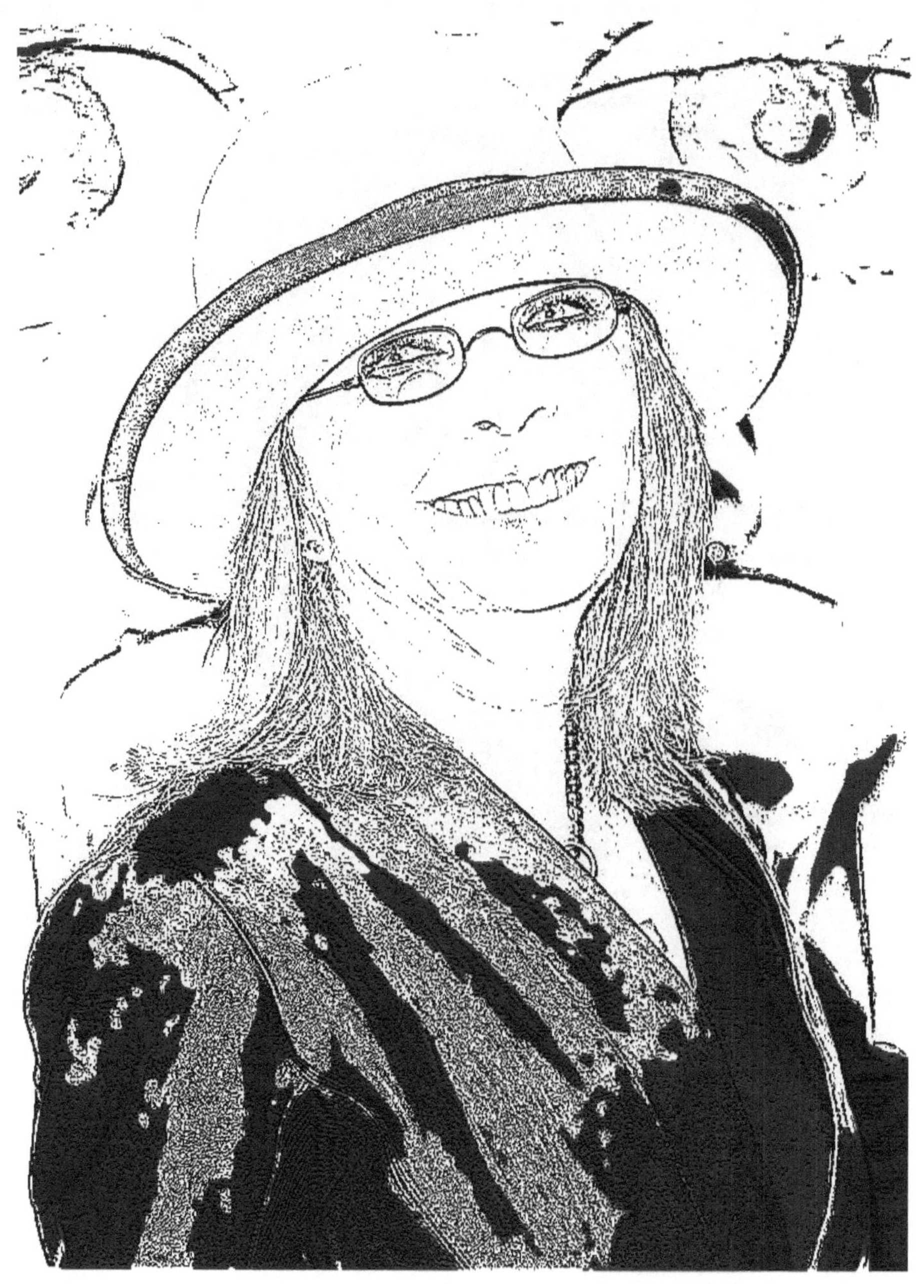

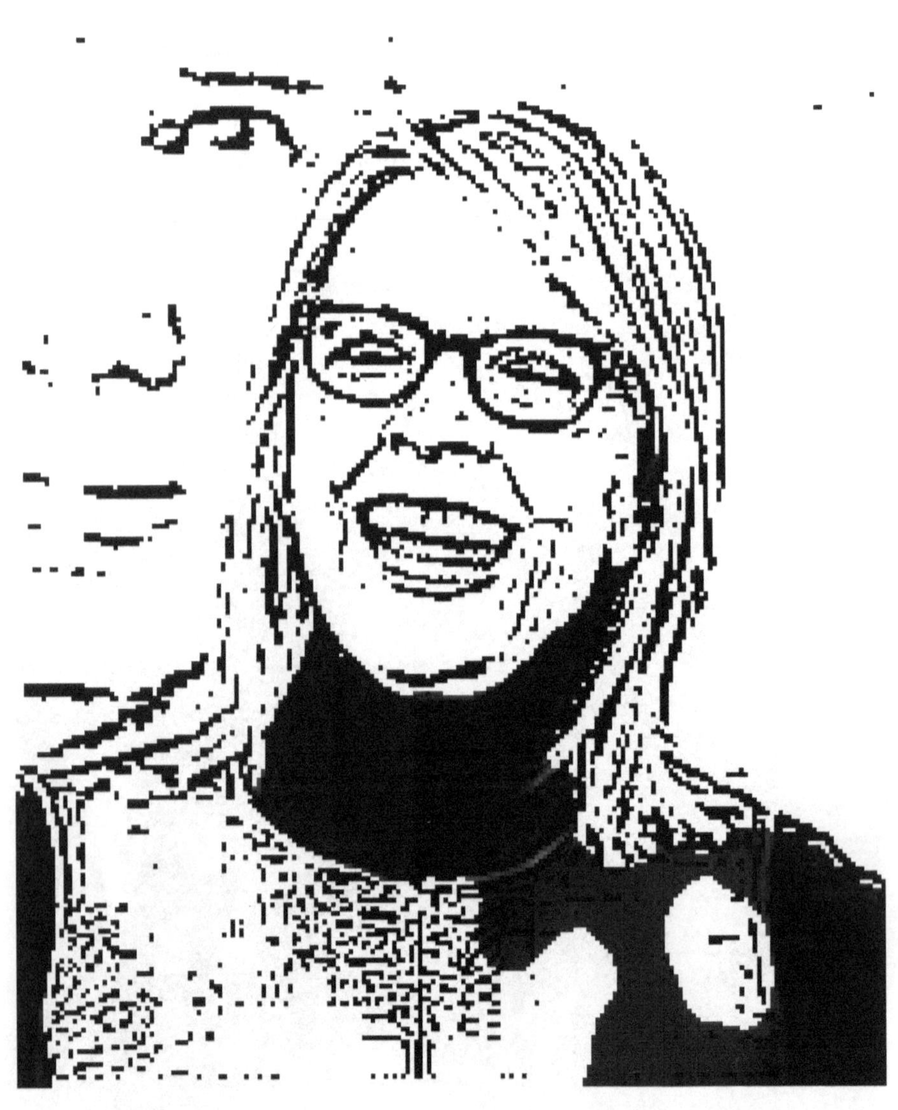

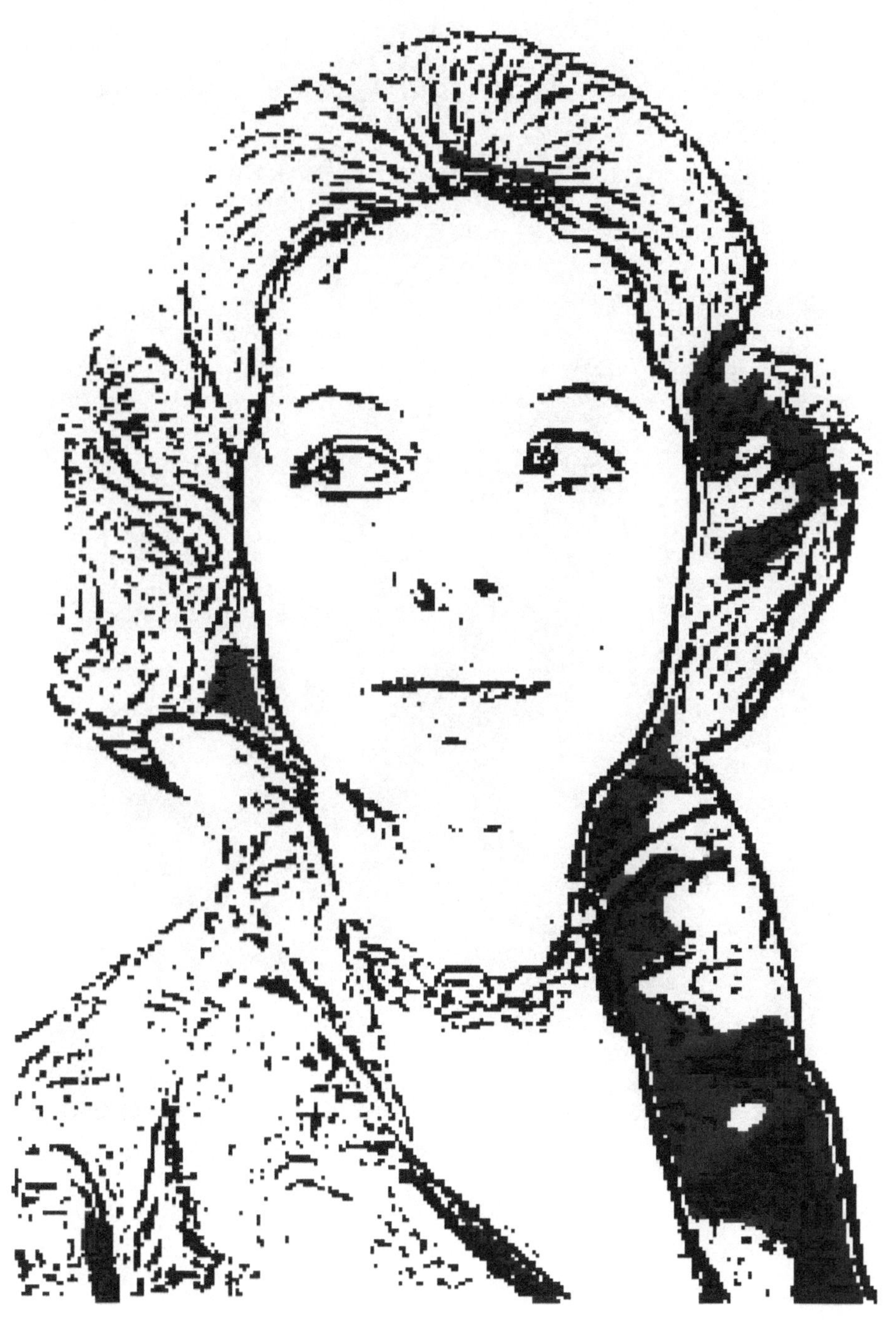

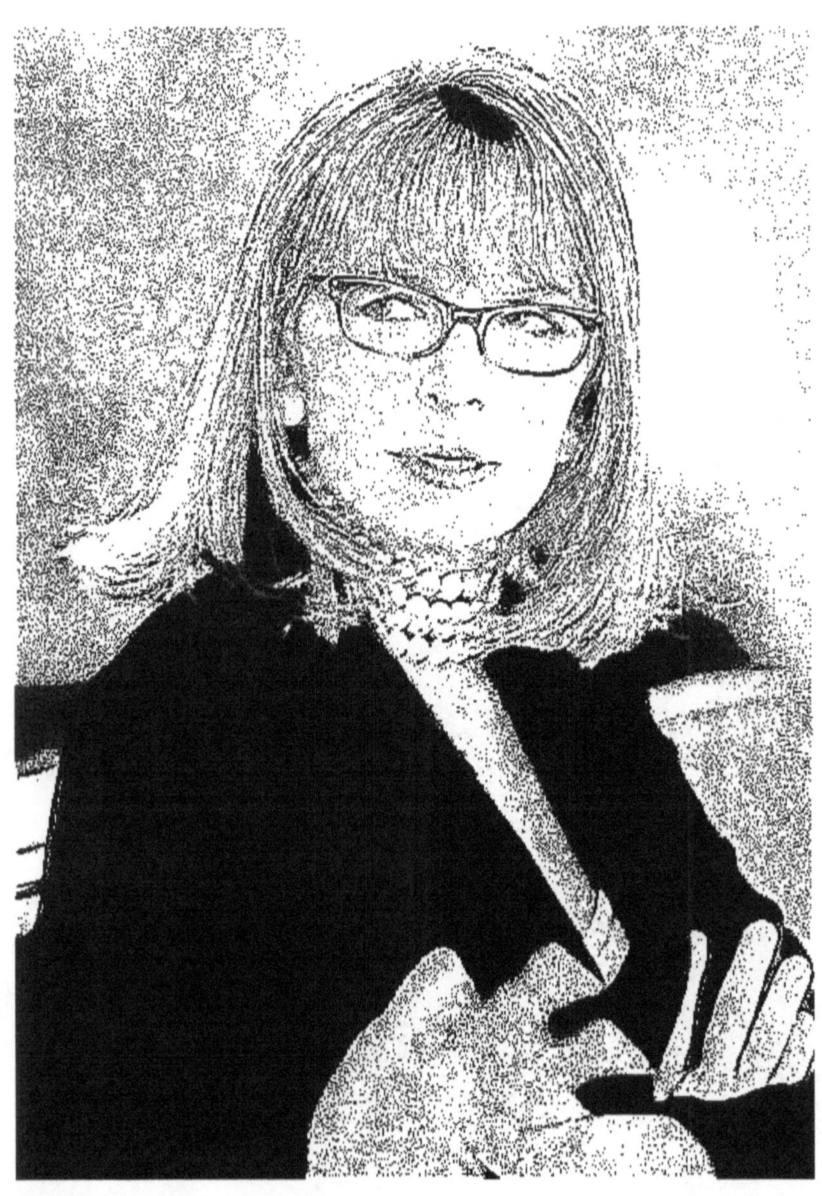

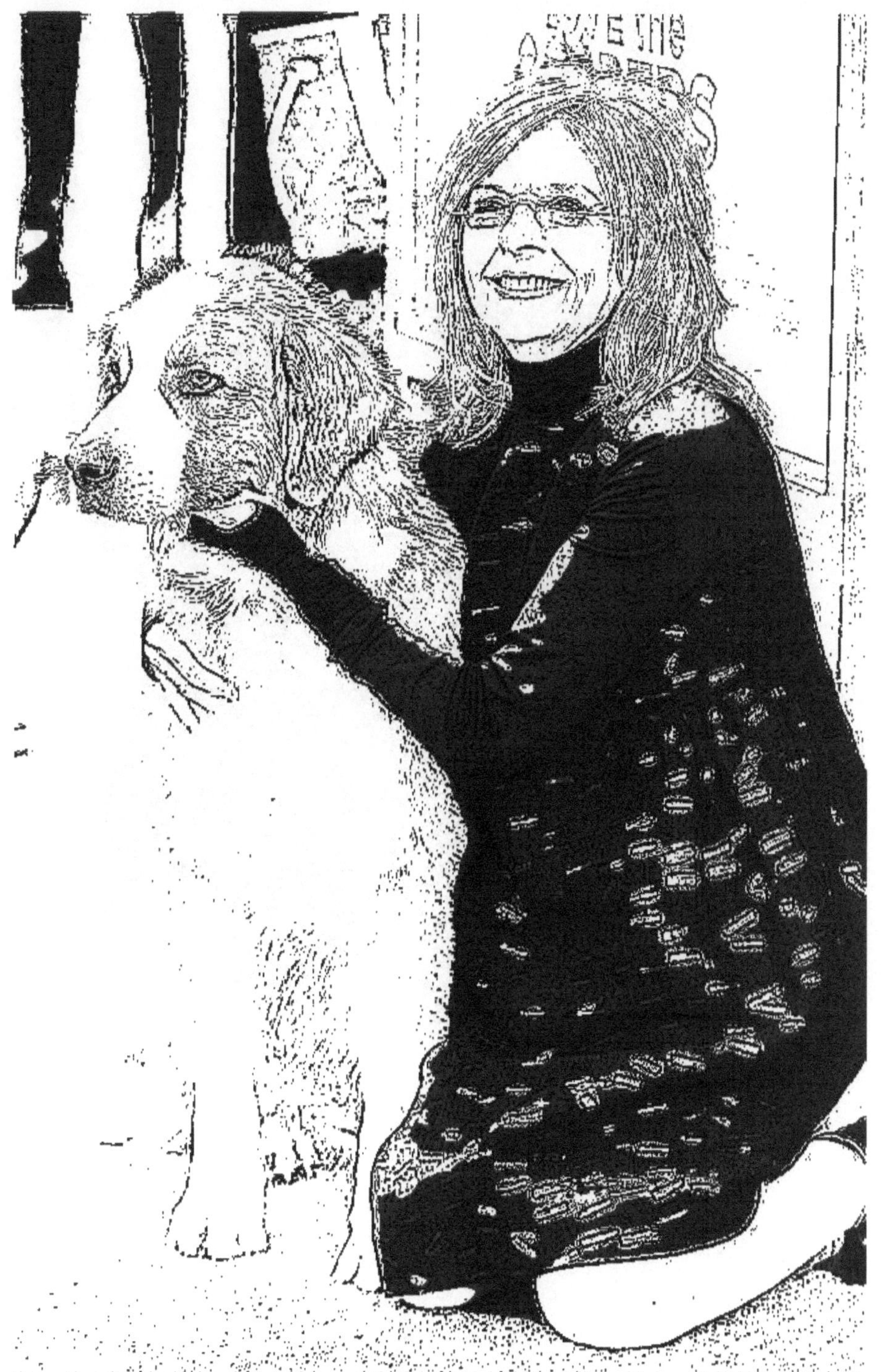

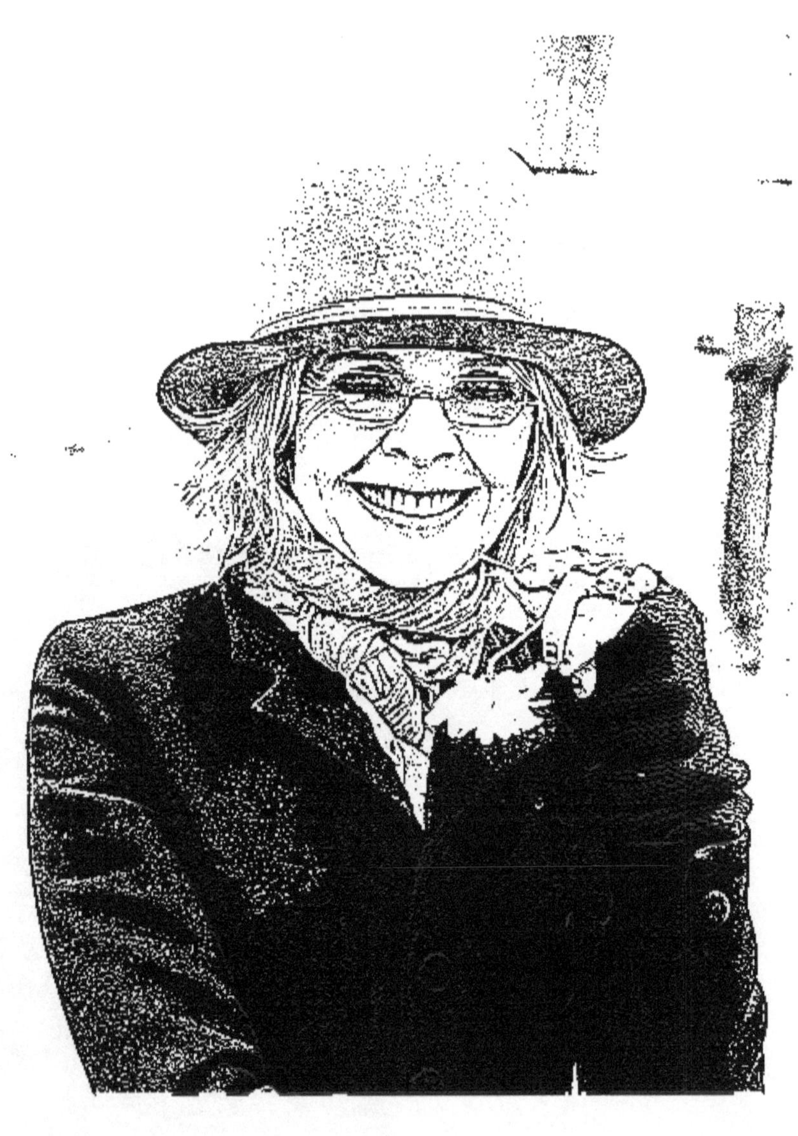

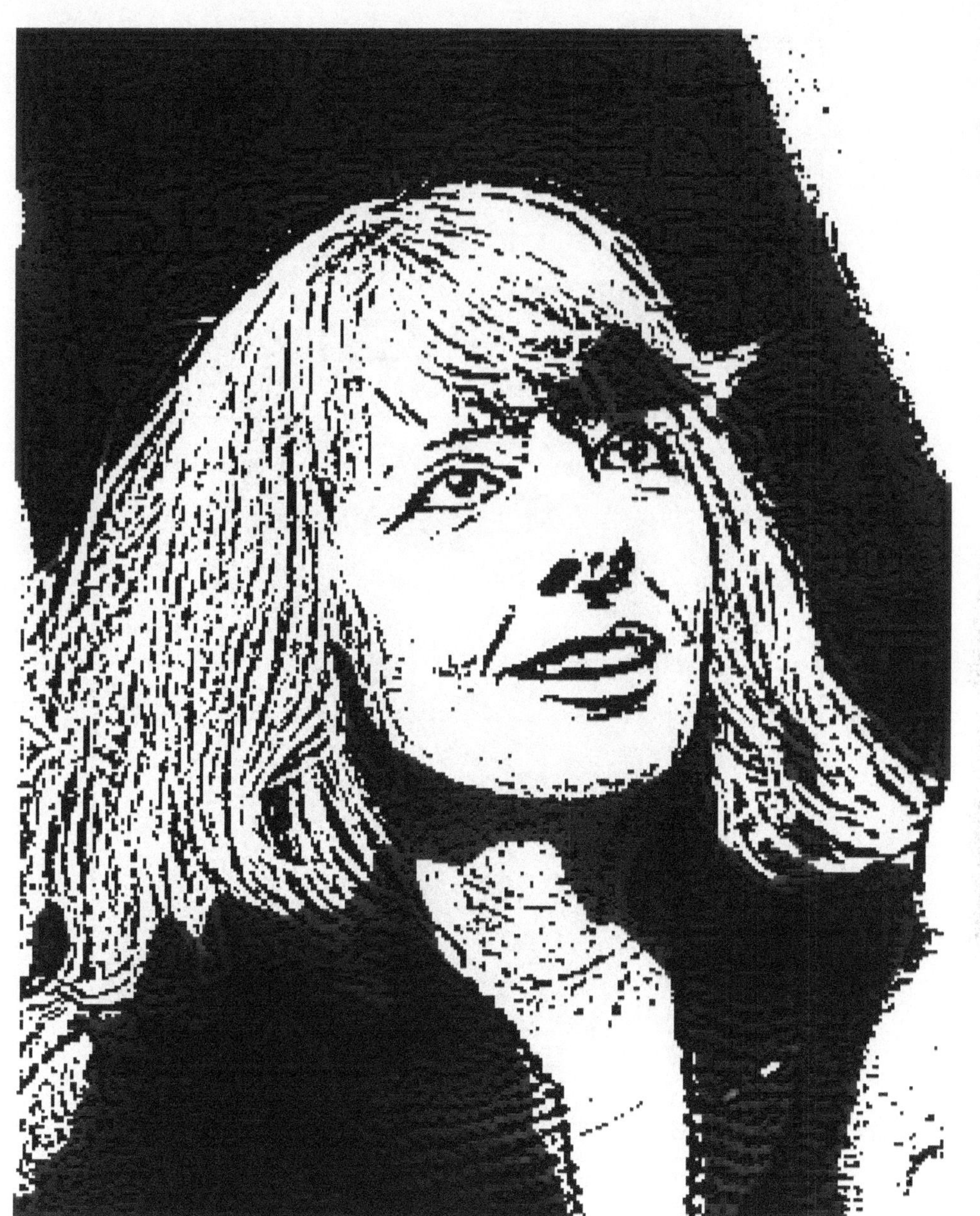

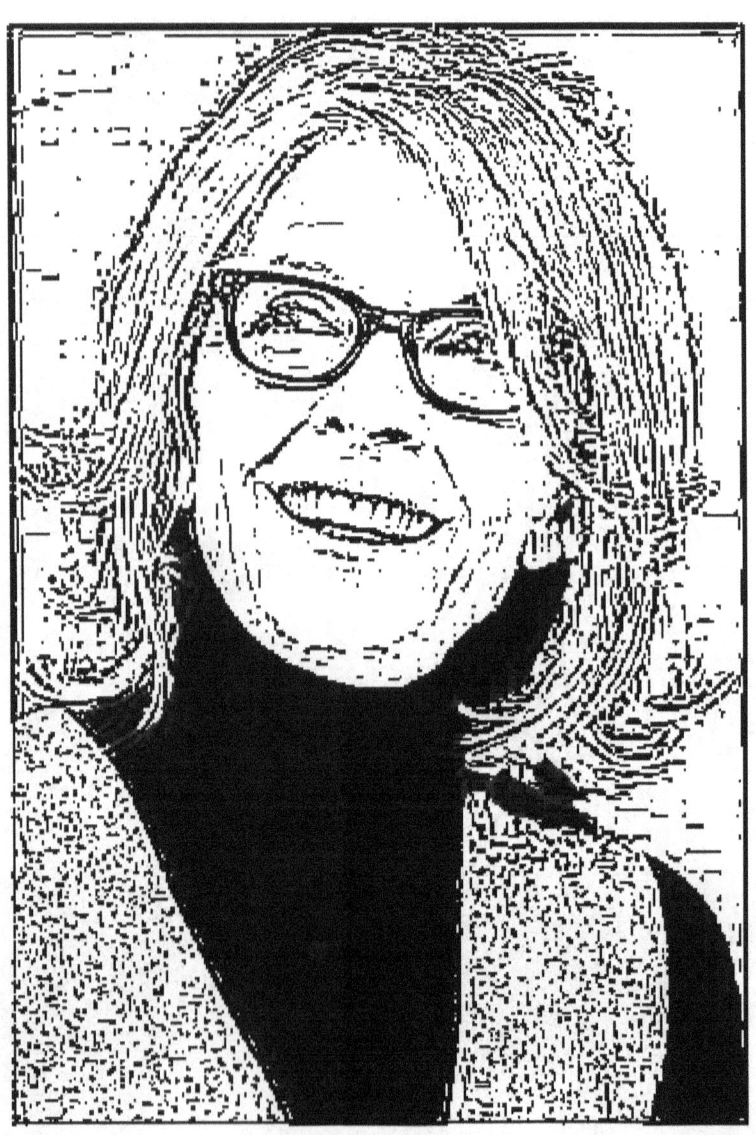

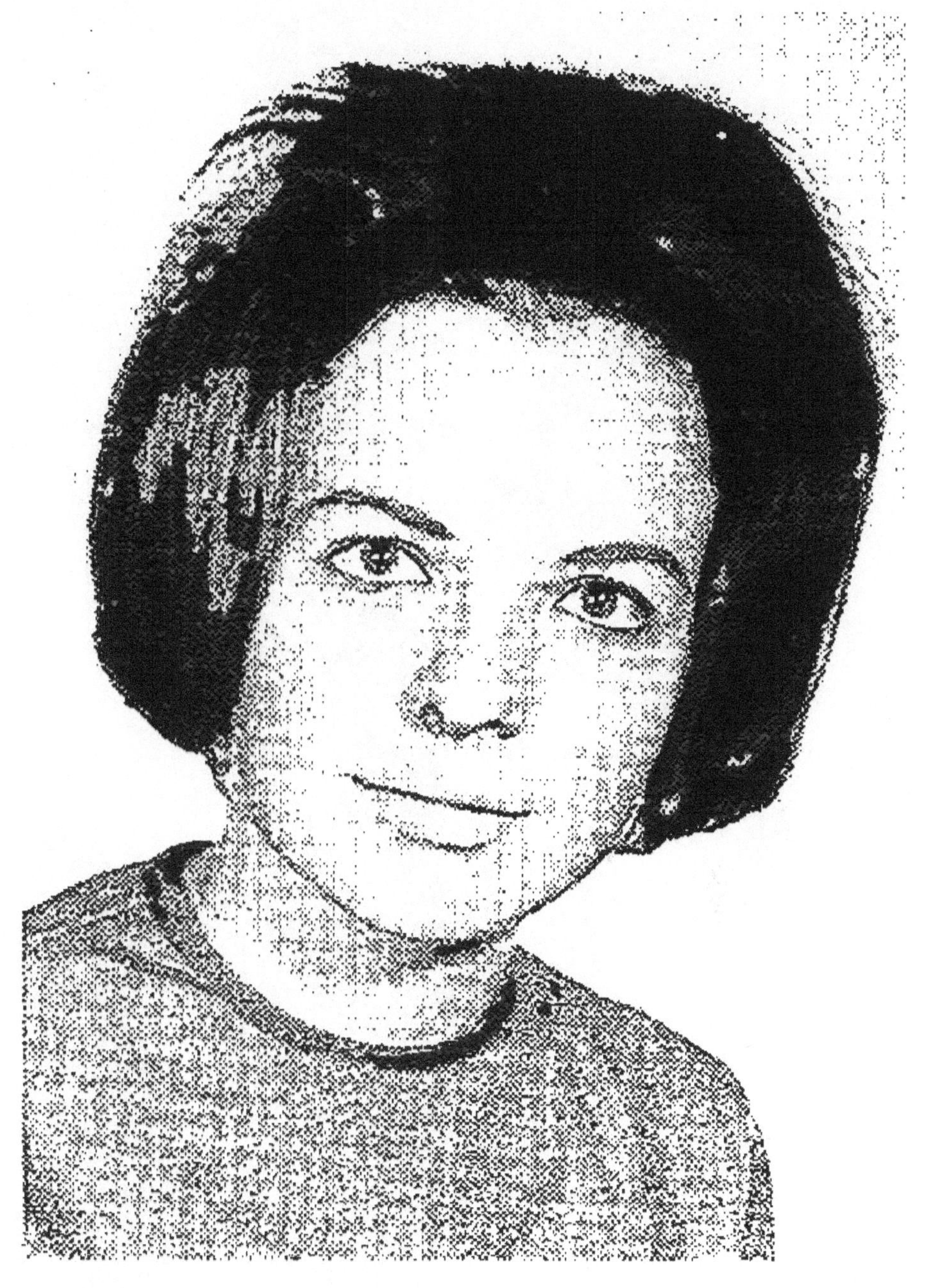

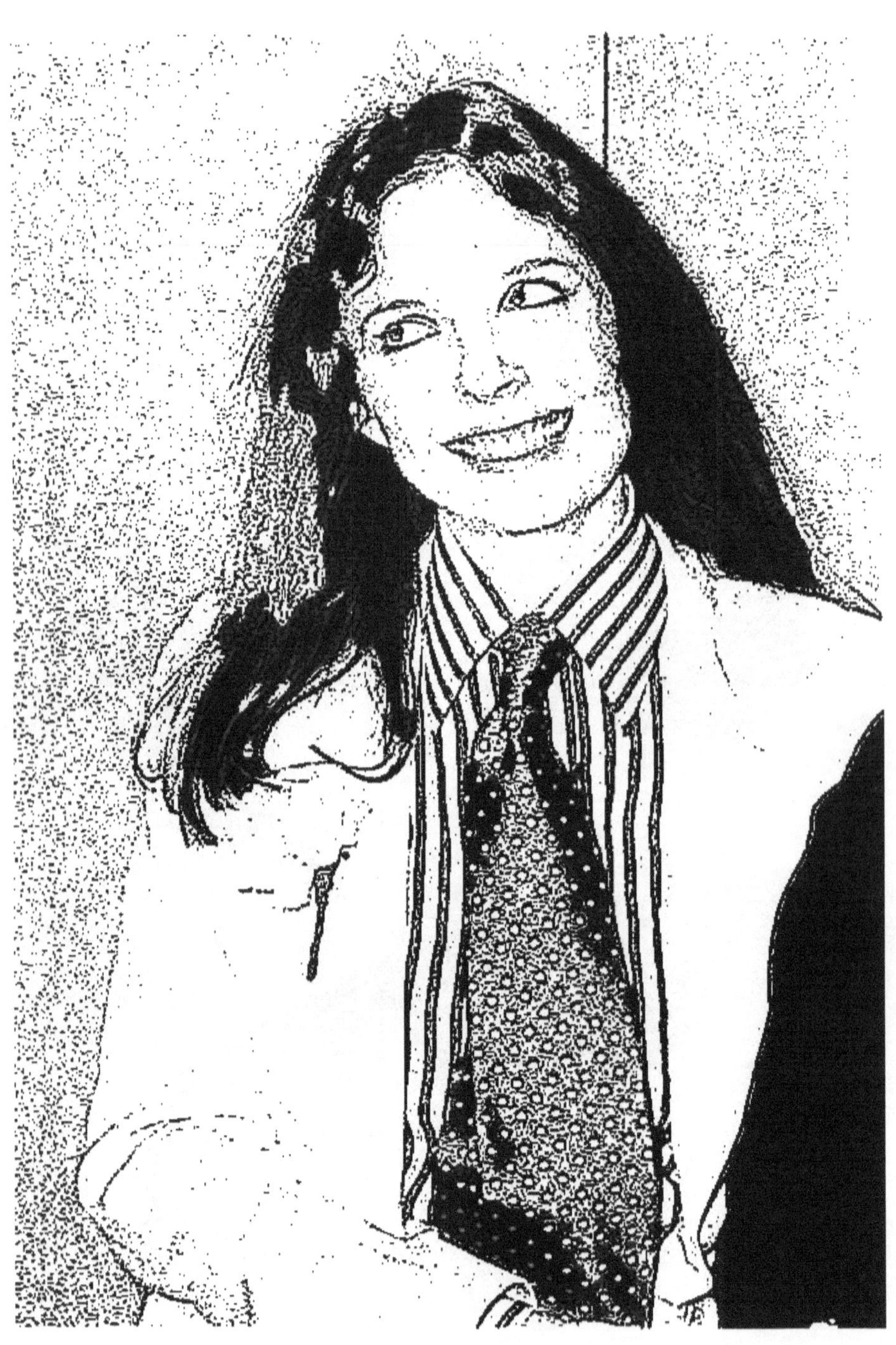

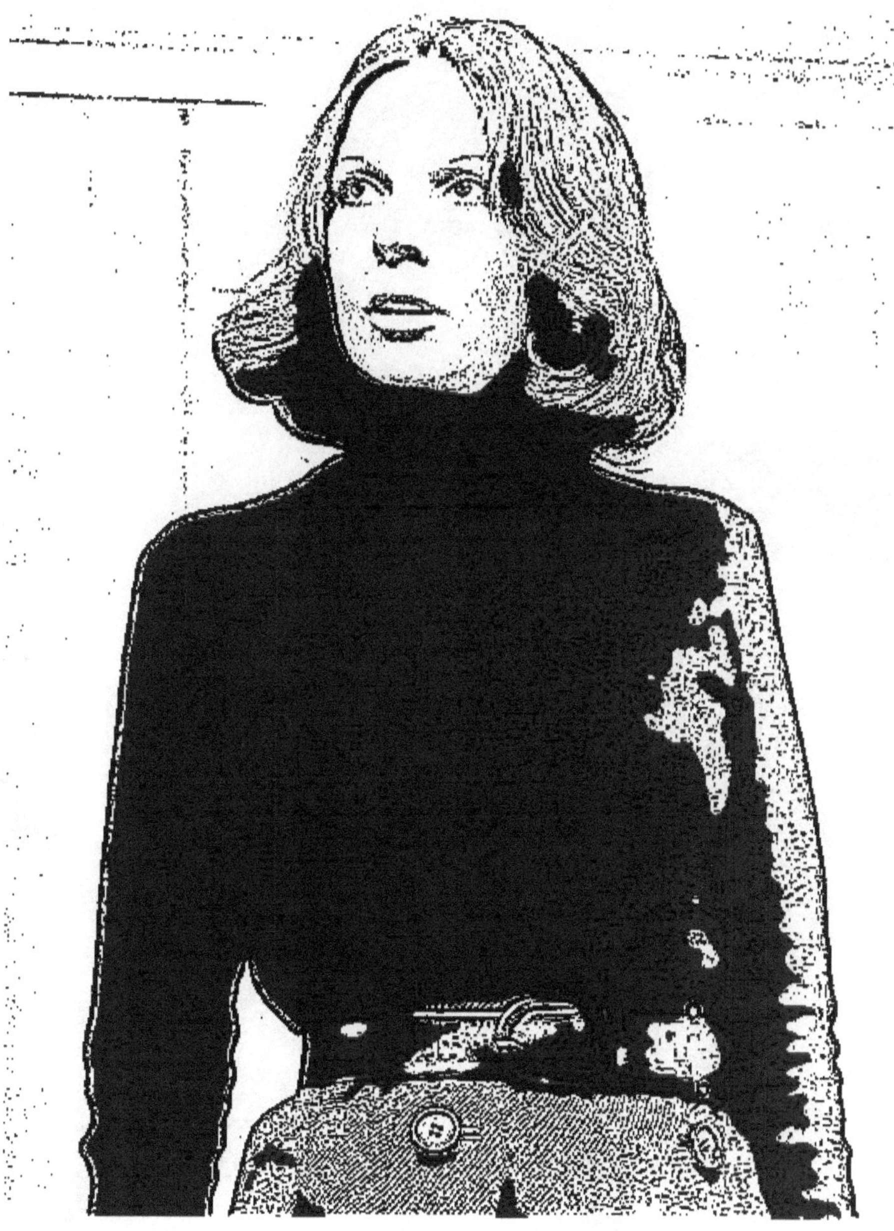

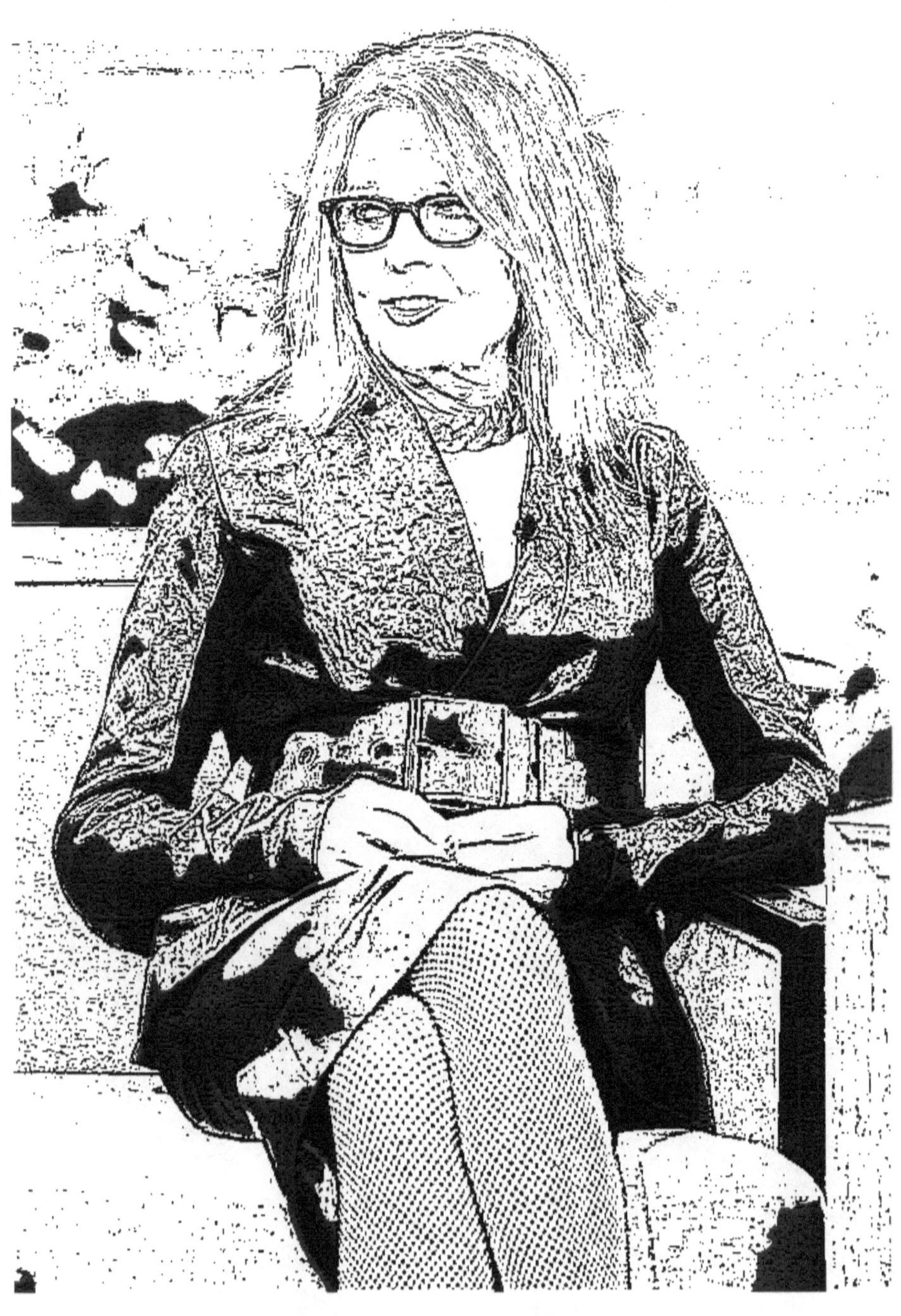

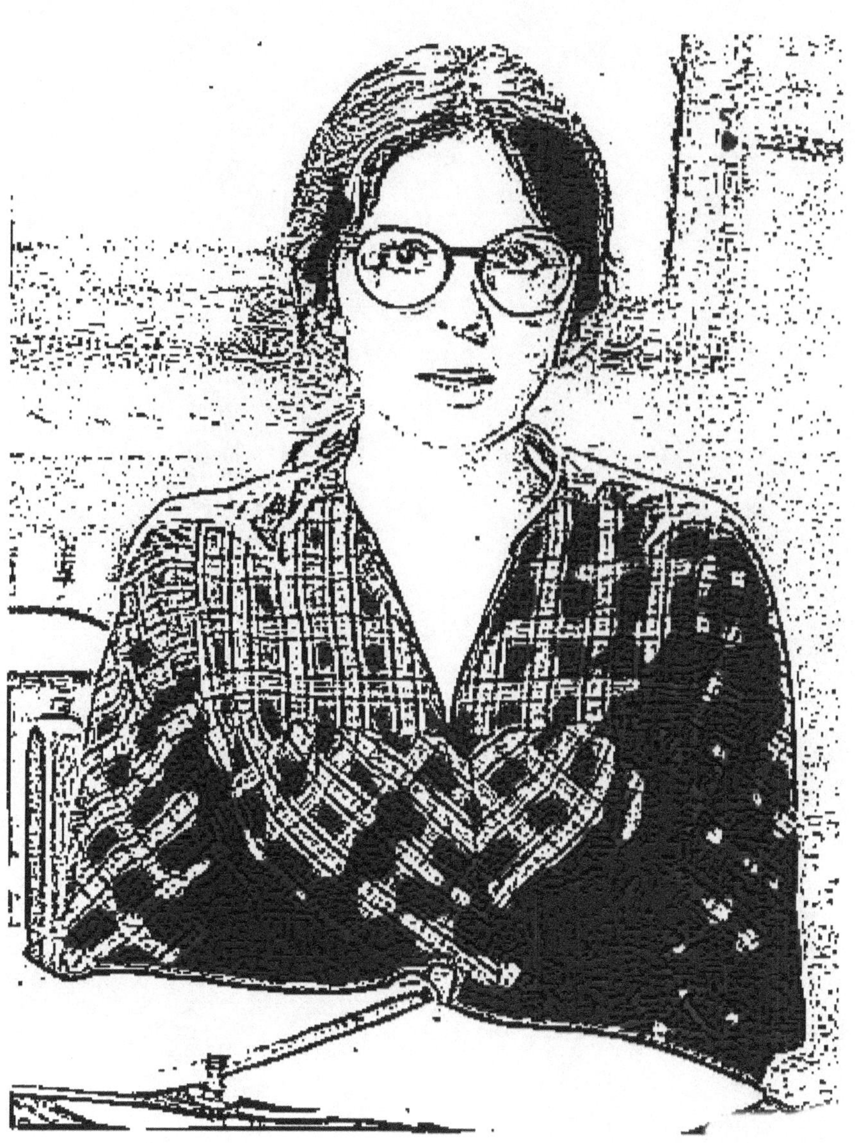

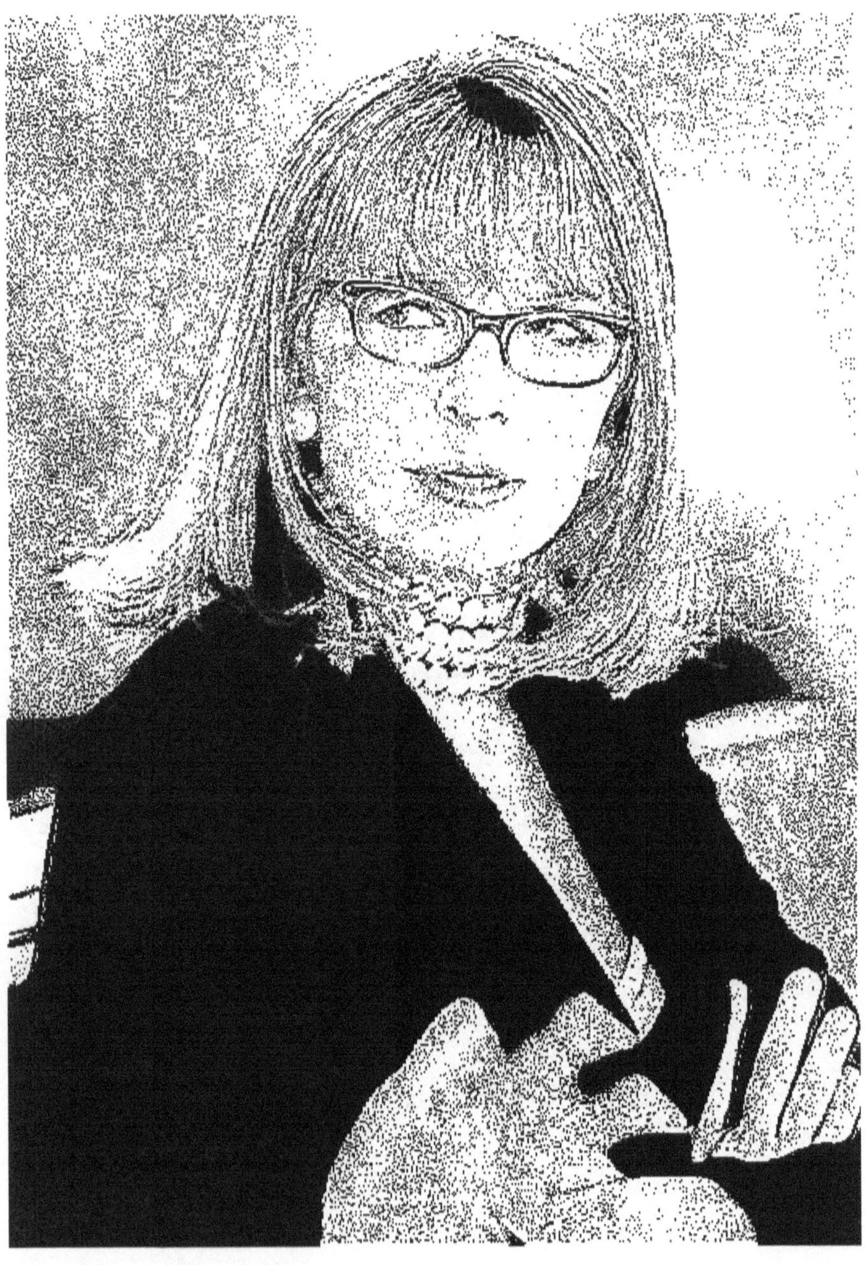